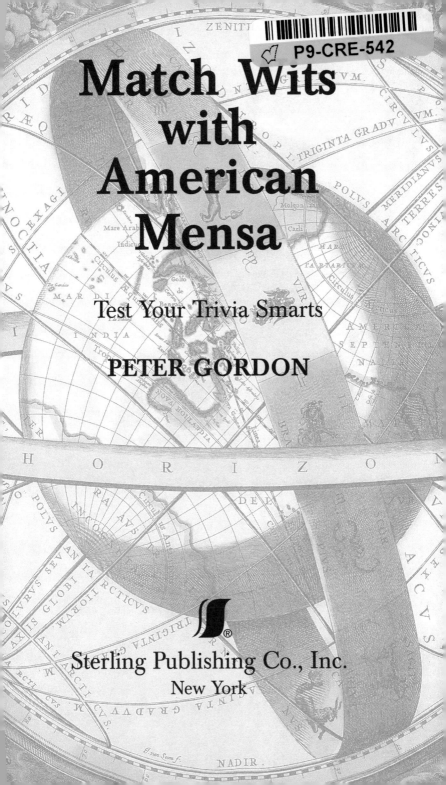

Match Wits with American Mensa

Test Your Trivia Smarts

PETER GORDON

Sterling Publishing Co., Inc.
New York

P9-CRE-542

For Chrissy,
who so gracefully puts up with all my trivialities

Library of Congress Cataloging-in-Publication Data
Gordon, Peter, 1966–
    Match wits with American Mensa : test your trivia
smarts / Peter Gordon.
        p.   cm.
    Includes index.
    ISBN 0-8069-1243-X
    1. Questions and answers. I. Title.
AG195.G66   1999
031.02–dc21

                      99-39743
                      CIP

10 9 8 7 6 5 4 3 2 1

Published by Sterling Publishing Company, Inc.
387 Park Avenue South, New York, N.Y. 10016
© 1999 by Peter Gordon
Distributed in Canada by Sterling Publishing
%Canadian Manda Group, One Atlantic Avenue, Suite 105
Toronto, Ontario, Canada M6K 3E7
Distributed in Great Britain and Europe by Cassell PLC
Wellington House, 125 Strand, London WC2R 0BB, England
Distributed in Australia by Capricorn Link (Australia) Pty Ltd.
P.O. Box 6651, Baulkham Hills, Business Centre,
NSW 2153, Australia
Manufactured in the United States of America

Sterling ISBN 0-8069-1243-X

Contents

Introduction   4

Movies and Television   7

1. 9	3. 11	5. 13	7. 15	9. 17
2. 10	4. 12	6. 14	8. 16	10. 18

Music, Arts, and Letters   19

1. 21	3. 23	5. 25	7. 27	9. 29
2. 22	4. 24	6. 26	8. 28	10. 30

Sports and Games   31

1. 33	3. 35	5. 37	7. 39	9. 41
2. 34	4. 36	6. 38	8. 40	10. 42

Travel and Geography   43

1. 45	3. 47	5. 49	7. 51	9. 53
2. 46	4. 48	6. 50	8. 52	10. 54

History and Science   55

1. 57	3. 59	5. 61	7. 63	9. 65
2. 58	4. 60	6. 62	8. 64	10. 66

Brainbusters   67
(Each of the questions in these two tests were *missed* by more than 90% of Mensa members! Can you answer them?)

Answers   69

Index   87

What Is American Mensa?   96

Introduction

Are you a trivia genius? You're about to find out. Here are 520 trivia questions in five different categories: Movies and Television; Music, Arts, and Letters; Sports and Games; Travel and Geography; and History and Science. (To make it easy to fit into your busy schedules, the questions have been broken down into ten 10-question trivia tests in each category, plus two 10-question "Brainbusters," made up of the most-missed questions.)

Every question was sent to forty members of American Mensa (the High IQ Society) who had expressed interest in trivia or puzzles. Their answers were graded, and the questions in each category are presented in order of difficulty, based on these responses. In addition to providing the answers, we indicate what percentage of our Mensa members got each question correct. So now you can compare yourself to the "cream of the crop," based on running total or on each question. What does it mean if you consistently do better than the average Mensa member? It probably means that people who like to win don't like to play trivia games with you. Welcome to the club.

For the purposes of scoring, each question counts for one point. To count as correct, all parts of the answer must be right. If the question asks for two names, both must be correct to score the point. There is no partial credit. For the names of real people, only the last name is required. For fictional names, either the first or last name is enough. For cities, you need only the city name, not the state or country where the city is found. Any portion of the answer in parentheses is there for clarification, and is not required for your answer to count as correct. There is no penalty for wrong answers.

The Mensa members had to work alone and were not allowed to use any references. You can cheat as much as you feel comfortable with.

Two 10-question "Brainbusters" appear at the back of the testing section. These are questions that only two or three of the forty Mensa members got right. If you can answer two or more of these 20 questions correctly, you may just be a trivia genius.

Special thanks to the following forty Mensa members, whose scores you will be going up against: Beth S. Agejew, Howie Asaki, Alan E. Baltis, Patty Buethe, Donna Spencer Bognar, Monica Bohonko, Vince Bonzagni, Jerry Breuer, Pete M. Brown, Dan Burg, Cher Burnham, Jeff Bussell, Joan Forgrave Carter, Brian Corbishley, James E. Couture, Kathy Crum, Jay-Jay Flanagan-Grannemann, Irv Freeman, Dr. Tara Lenore Gilmore, Deborah Henry, Susan K. Henthorn, Steve Herrick, Matthew Kamin, Marcia King, Lyn Lynn, Shelley MacGregor, Charles R. Martinez, Ilene McGrath, Bob Murrin, John B. Nash, Rodney Ruff, Miriam Schneidmill, John Stephen Singer, Allison Stallings, Barbara A. Steiner, Karen S. Steiner, Kevin Stewart, William W. Travis, Joe Vaughan, and Steven F. Yaros.

—Peter Gordon

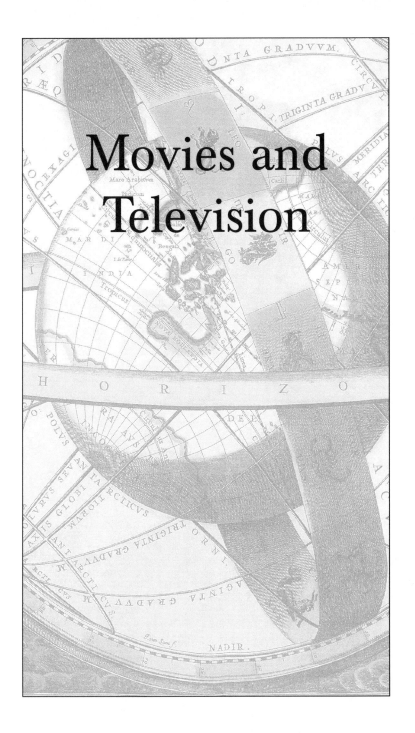

Movies and
Television

Movies and Television

1 What are the names of Donald Duck's three nephews?

2 What newspaper did Clark Kent and Lois Lane work for?

3 Kids' TV show host Bob Keeshan is better known by what name?

4 On *Star Trek*, what is the color of Mr. Spock's blood?

5 Tinky Winky, Laa-Laa, Po, and Dipsy are collectively known as what?

6 What TV series had, as a part of the plot, a TV show called *Tool Time*?

7 Which *60 Minutes* correspondent wears an earring?
a) Mike Wallace b) Morley Safer
c) Ed Bradley d) Andy Rooney

8 What movie had a sequel entitled *Oliver's Story*?

9 What TV star of the 1960s had a valet named Rochester?

10 What regular from *The Bob Newhart Show* made a guest appearance in the final scene of the final episode of *Newhart*?

Answers on page 70.

MENSA SCORING	
Average Mensa score:	8.525
Cumulative Mensa score in this category:	8.525

Movies and Television

11 What actor was reelected mayor of Carmel, California, in 1988?

12 What action star is nicknamed "Muscles from Brussels"?

13 What is Kramer's first name on *Seinfeld*?

14 What show's final episode was titled "Goodbye, Farewell, Amen"?

15 In an episode of what series did the character of Mork, later of *Mork & Mindy* fame, first appear?

16 What Oscar-winning actress is sister to Warren Beatty?

17 What talk show host was once mayor of Cincinnati?

18 What Oscar-winning actress played Janet in *The Rocky Horror Picture Show*?

19 What state was the setting for the TV series *I Dream of Jeannie*?

20 Who is the title character in *The Fugitive*?

Answers on page 70.

MENSA SCORING	
Average Mensa score:	7.15
Cumulative Mensa score in this category:	15.675

Movies and Television

21 Name the character played by Flip Wilson in drag whose boyfriend was named Killer.

22 What actress won the 1997 Oscar for Best Actress and the 1996–97 Emmy for Best Actress in a Comedy Series?

23 What was the movie shown that day in 1968 when NBC cut away from a football game between the Oakland Raiders and New York Jets with 50 seconds to go, and the Raiders took the lead by scoring two touchdowns?

24 What is the name of the first sound cartoon film featuring Mickey Mouse?

25 On the series *M*A*S*H*, what is Radar's favorite drink?

26 What Scottish actor represented Scotland in 1950 at London's Mr. Universe competition?

27 What actor changed his name from Archibald Leach?

28 Name the six children on *The Brady Bunch.*

29 What noted director is well known for playing clarinet in a Dixie jazz band Monday nights in Manhattan?

30 What was the name of the doorman on *Rhoda*?

Answers on page 71.

MENSA SCORING	
Average Mensa score:	6.45
Cumulative Mensa score in this category:	22.125

Movies and Television

31 Who is Gwyneth Paltrow's mother?

32 What is the only movie sequel to win the Oscar for Best Picture?

33 What was the first name of Norm's wife on *Cheers*?

34 What was Lucy Ricardo's maiden name on *I Love Lucy*?

35 What special feature, designed for the movie *Earthquake*, allowed viewers to "feel" the vibrations?

36 Who was originally cast as Catwoman in *Batman Returns* but lost the role when she got pregnant?
a) Elisabeth Shue b) Annette Bening
c) Sigourney Weaver d) Geena Davis

37 What was the name of the souped-up Dodge Charger in *The Dukes of Hazzard*?

38 Who speaks the only word in Mel Brooks's 1976 comedy *Silent Movie*?

39 What three TV series were spun off from *The Mary Tyler Moore Show*?

40 Who directed the PBS documentary *The Civil War*?

Answers on page 71.

Movies and Television   5

41 Who won an Oscar for Best Director in his directorial debut, *Ordinary People*?

42 What movie begins with Annie Savoy saying, as the first line of the script, "I believe in the Church of Baseball"?

43 What actor on the original TV show *The Love Boat* was elected to the U.S. Congress?

44 What are the names of the Blues Brothers?

45 Who is Jane Pauley's husband?

46 Who gave Elizabeth Taylor away at her marriage to Larry Fortensky?

47 What actress bought the town of Braselton, Georgia, for $20 million in 1989?

48 Who was first runner-up in the 1986 Miss USA pageant?
a) Halle Berry b) Calista Flockhart
c) Cindy Crawford d) Cameron Diaz

49 What TV personality won over $100,000 on *The $64,000 Question* and *The $64,000 Challenge* on the topic of boxing?

50 In *The Wizard of Oz*, what is Dorothy's last name?

Answers on page 71.

MENSA SCORING	
Average Mensa score:	4.875
Cumulative Mensa score in this category:	32.45

Movies and Television

51 On what TV show did characters hang out at the Regal Beagle?

52 What actress provided the speaking voice of Jessica Rabbit in *Who Framed Roger Rabbit*?

53 What television series featured two Englishwomen named Cecily and Gwendolyn Pigeon as apartment house neighbors?

54 What talk show was originally known as *A.M. Chicago*?

55 What 1978 movie was a remake of the 1941 movie *Here Comes Mr. Jordan*?

56 What's the only X-rated film to win Best Picture?

57 On the show *Frasier*, what breed of dog is Eddie?

58 In what magazine did Burt Reynolds, in 1972, pose nude for the centerfold?

59 What actor, who later won an Oscar for Best Director, appeared only as the corpse in the opening credits of *The Big Chill* after all his other scenes in the movie were cut?

60 What film is noted as being the final one for both Clark Gable and Marilyn Monroe?

Answers on page 71.

MENSA SCORING	
Average Mensa score:	4.475
Cumulative Mensa score in this category:	36.925

Movies and Television 7

61 Who is Melanie Griffith's mother?

62 What TV show has the theme song "Keep Your Eye on the Sparrow"?

63 What's the name of the production company that produces *Late Show with David Letterman*?

64 What fictional name do directors put on films when they don't want their names to appear?
a) Ogden Porter b) Roger Bollinger
c) Alan Smithee d) Chris Covell

65 What TV family lived at 1313 Mockingbird Lane?

66 Who sang a love song to Johnny Carson on his next-to-last show as host of *The Tonight Show*?

67 What is the registration number of the *Enterprise*, following "NCC" on the hull, in the original *Star Trek* series?

68 What TV series had *Cyborg* as a working title?

69 Two actresses tied for Best Actress in 1968. Name either.

70 What is the name of Dale Evans's horse?

Answers on page 72.

MENSA SCORING	
Average Mensa score:	3.775
Cumulative Mensa score in this category:	40.7

Movies and Television

71 Which of the following performed the marriage of Bruce Willis and Demi Moore?
a) Peter Jennings b) Jerry Falwell
c) Little Richard d) Deepak Chopra

72 Telly Savalas is godfather to which *Friends* star?

73 What is the longest-running series in television history?

74 In the original Motion Picture Association of America rating system, what was the fourth designation letter used, besides G, R, and X?

75 What Oscar-winning actor was Al Gore's roommate at Harvard?

76 In the Marx Brothers' film *Duck Soup*, Rufus T. Firefly rules what fictional country?

77 Who played a doctor in the short-lived CBS series *E/R* and also in the hit NBC series *ER*?

78 What is ALF's home planet?

79 What band took its name from a character in the film *Barbarella*?

80 What movie had *Made Men* as a working title?

Answers on page 72.

MENSA SCORING	
Average Mensa score:	3.025
Cumulative Mensa score in this category:	43.725

Movies and Television 9

81 What is the name of the estate in *Citizen Kane?*

82 What state did Vanessa Williams represent when she won the 1984 Miss America pageant?

83 What Woody Allen movie was a Japanese movie that was redubbed to be about a valuable egg salad recipe?

84 Who collaborated with Johnny Carson to write "Johnny's Theme," the theme song to *The Tonight Show Starring Johnny Carson?*

85 Name the two actors who starred opposite each other in the movie *Sleuth.*

86 What Oscar-winning actor is nephew to Talia Shire?

87 What movie was based on the Phillip K. Dick short story "We Can Remember It for You Wholesale"?

88 Who married Ethan Hawke in 1998?

89 What saying did Jack Nicholson's character type over and over in *The Shining?*

90 What do the letters SKG stand for in Dreamworks SKG?

Answers on page 72.

MENSA SCORING

Average Mensa score:	2.4
Cumulative Mensa score in this category:	46.125

Movies and Television

91 Who supplies the voice of Li'l Penny in Nike ads?

92 What two films won 11 Oscars?

93 What actress started the film production company Egg Pictures?

94 The words "in the Clair de Lune" were dropped from the end of the title of what film based on a Terrence McNally play?

95 Three movies to date have won all five major Oscars (picture, director, actor, actress, and screenplay). Name two.

96 Two Best Picture winners have had abbreviations in their titles. Name either.

97 In 1972, one film had three actors nominated for Best Supporting Actor and one actor nominated for Best Actor. Name the film and the actors.

98 What movie is noted for the film debut of both Drew Barrymore and William Hurt?

99 What movie title completes the following line from the film: "Don't you agree that on one's first visit to Florence one must have ___?"

100 What is Mr. Magoo's first name?

Answers on page 72.

MENSA SCORING	
Average Mensa score:	1.375
Cumulative Mensa score in this category:	47.5

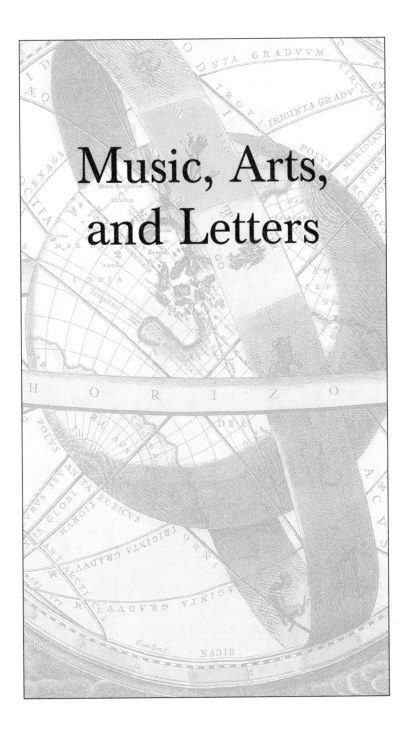

Music, Arts,
and Letters

Music, Arts, and Letters

1 What are the last names of the feuding families in *Romeo and Juliet*?

2 What is the final word of "The Raven"?

3 How many keys are on a standard piano?

4 According to song, what train leaves from track 29 at Pennsylvania Station at about a quarter to four?

5 What Shakespearean play features the character Shylock, a moneylender?

6 What's the name of the title character in *The Hunchback of Notre Dame*?

7 In ballet, what is the bending-of-the-knees movement?

8 What is the slogan of *The New York Times* (it appears in the upper left corner of every front page)?

9 What singer was named Robert Zimmerman at birth?

10 What are the two cities in *A Tale of Two Cities*?

Answers on page 73.

MUSIC/ARTS/LETTERS

MENSA SCORING	
Average Mensa score:	7.95
Cumulative Mensa score in this category:	7.95

Music, Arts, and Letters

11 Who wrote *The Andromeda Strain*?

12 What three famous singers died in an airplane crash on February 3, 1959?

13 What is the third book of the Bible?

14 What musical period came between the Renaissance and Classical periods?

15 Who read the poem "I Shall Not Be Moved" at Bill Clinton's first inauguration?

16 What singer changed his name from Reginald Dwight?

17 What war is depicted in Pablo Picasso's *Guernica*?

18 Which of the following titles is not a line from Shakespeare?
   a) *The Catcher in the Rye* by J.D. Salinger
   b) *Brave New World* by Aldous Huxley
   c) *Something Wicked This Way Comes* by Ray Bradbury
   d) *The Winter of Our Discontent* by John Steinbeck

19 Simon Legree is the villain in what novel?

20 What best-selling author sometimes writes under the pseudonym Richard Bachman?

Answers on page 73.

MENSA SCORING

Average Mensa score:	6.325
Cumulative Mensa score in this category:	14.275

Music, Arts, and Letters

21 What musical is based on the story of Christopher Isherwood's *Goodbye to Berlin*?

22 What is the longest-running play in London?

23 What is the longest-running show in Broadway history?

24 How many syllables are typically in a haiku?

25 The mythical creature called the griffin is made up of what two animals?

26 What singer led the Mothers of Invention?

27 Which three U.S. states are titles of books by James A. Michener?

28 Who painted *Impression: Sunrise*, the painting that gave impressionism its name?

29 What rock star died in a bathtub in Paris on July 3, 1971?

30 Who painted *American Gothic*?

Answers on page 74.

MENSA SCORING	
Average Mensa score:	5.275
Cumulative Mensa score in this category:	19.55

Music, Arts, and Letters

31 Who holds the record for being on the most covers of *People*?

32 What is Tom Sawyer's aunt's name?

33 What singing group had Fabrice Morvan and Rob Pilatus as its members?

34 What mythological figure is condemned to roll a huge stone up a hill, only to have it roll down again each time?

35 Georges Seurat's *Sunday Afternoon on the Island of La Grande Jatte* is one of the best-known examples of what painting style?

36 What was the name of the town through which Lady Godiva rode naked?

37 What magazine has regular departments that include "Letters and Tomatoes" and "Joke and Dagger"?

38 Who is the author of the *Goosebumps* series of children's books?

39 What science fiction story features the Morlocks and the Eloi?

40 Who created Sam Spade?

Answers on page 74.

MENSA SCORING

Average Mensa score:	4.5
Cumulative Mensa score in this category:	24.05

Music, Arts, and Letters

41 What city is home to the Uffizi Gallery?

42 What author set many of his novels in fictional Yokna-patawpha County?

43 Name the four other original "spices" besides Ginger Spice in the Spice Girls?

44 Who was the third tenor, besides Luciano Pavarotti and Placido Domingo, on the Three Tenors album?

45 What's the name of the three-headed dog that guards the entrance to Hades?

46 What is the name of the famous art museum in St. Petersburg, Russia?

47 What university administers the Pulitzer Prize awards?

48 Who wrote *The Night of the Iguana*?

49 What is the Greek name of the Roman god Minerva?

50 What opera is the musical *Rent* based on?

Answers on page 74.

MENSA SCORING	
Average Mensa score:	3.875
Cumulative Mensa score in this category:	27.925

Music, Arts, and Letters

51 In the Gustave Flaubert novel, what is the first name of *Madame Bovary*?

52 Mitch McDeere is the main character in what best-selling novel?

53 Who wrote the book *Chitty Chitty Bang Bang*?

54 What is the more commonly known name of Franz Schubert's *Symphony No. 8 in B minor*?

55 The words "or the Modern Prometheus" are usually dropped from the title when discussing what 1818 novel?

56 What was the name of the dictatorial pig that ruled in *Animal Farm*?

57 What famous reporter wrote *Wired*, the biography of John Belushi?

58 What Russian writer died at the small railway junction of Astapovo during a train journey?

59 What modern dancer died when her scarf got caught in the tire of a moving car?

60 In what complex of buildings is the Metropolitan Opera located?

Answers on page 74.

MENSA SCORING	
Average Mensa score:	3.375
Cumulative Mensa score in this category:	31.3

Music, Arts, and Letters

61 What is the *Mona Lisa* called in Italian?

62 What's the name of the town in Thornton Wilder's *Our Town*?

63 What novelist features the fictional writer Kilgore Trout in several of his novels?

64 Who is the composer of *Pictures at an Exhibition*?

65 What was the London street address of Sherlock Holmes?

66 In the Sherlock Holmes stories, what is Dr. Watson's first name?

67 What musical opens with the song "Six Months out of Every Year"?

68 What are the names of King Lear's three daughters?

69 Who wrote *The Little Prince*?

70 What well-known American poet was married to English poet Ted Hughes?

Answers on page 75.

MUSIC/ARTS/LETTERS

MENSA SCORING	
Average Mensa score:	2.85
Cumulative Mensa score in this category:	34.15

Music, Arts, and Letters

71 Vladimir and Estragon are the two main characters in what play?

72 Who's the creator of the private investigator Kinsey Millhone?

73 Who wrote under the pen name Isak Dinesen?

74 Who designed and sculpted Mount Rushmore?

75 Which Beethoven symphony is known as Eroica?

76 Who designed the cover of Billy Joel's *River of Dreams* album?

77 Who designed the Rock and Roll Hall of Fame and Museum?

78 Who choreographed the dances for Broadway's *Oklahoma!*?

79 What daily newspaper has the highest weekday circulation in the country?

80 What actress rejected her 1996 Tony award nomination because her show wasn't nominated in any other category?

Answers on page 75.

Answers on page 75.

MENSA SCORING	
Average Mensa score:	2.55
Cumulative Mensa score in this category:	36.7

Music, Arts, and Letters

81 What farmer let his land be used for the Woodstock Festival in 1969?

82 Who appeared on the first *Rolling Stone* magazine cover?
a) Mick Jagger b) Elvis Presley
c) John Lennon d) Jimi Hendrix

83 What is the name of the poem by Emma Lazarus on the pedestal of the Statue of Liberty?

84 In *The World According to Garp*, what first and middle initial did Garp go by?

85 What's the name of B.B. King's guitar?

86 In *The Great Gatsby*, what's the name of the Long Island town where Jay Gatsby lives?

87 What band has a bassist named Flea?

88 Who is the Muse of history?

89 What novel begins, "It was a bright cold day in April, and the clocks were striking thirteen"?

90 What artist did several paintings of his wife, Gala?

Answers on page 75.

MUSIC/ARTS/LETTERS

MENSA SCORING	
Average Mensa score:	1.85
Cumulative Mensa score in this category:	38.55

Music, Arts, and Letters 10

91 Eustace Tilly appears annually on the cover of what magazine?

92 What three-letter name did Charles Dickens use as a pseudonym?

93 Who designed the famous Sagrada Familia church in Barcelona, Spain?

94 The novels *The 42nd Parallel*, *1919*, and *Big Money* make up what trilogy?

95 What was Jean Baptiste Poquelin's pen name?

96 What show featured the song "You're the Top"?

97 The character of Falstaff appears in three Shakespearean plays. Name two.

98 In what seven-part novel are the virtues of the French cake called a madeleine extolled?

99 What was Dr. Seuss's first published book?

100 What is Blondie Bumstead's maiden name?

Answers on page 75.

MENSA SCORING	
Average Mensa score:	1.2
Cumulative Mensa score in this category:	39.75

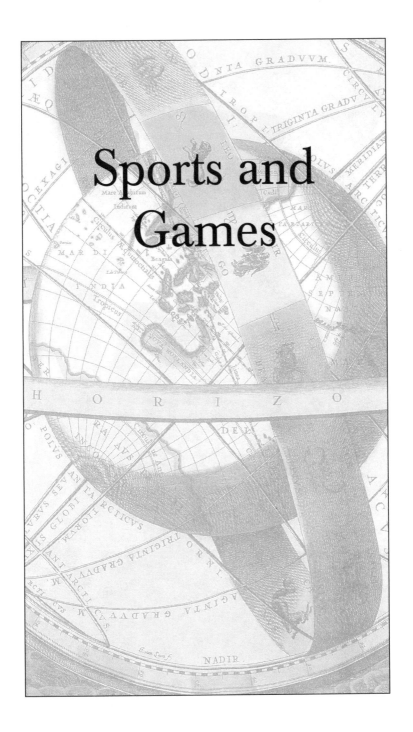

Sports and Games

Sports and Games

1 What Alaskan sled dog race goes from Anchorage to Nome?

2 In bowling, how many strikes are needed to bowl a perfect game?

3 What did Casey do in his turn at bat in the poem "Casey at the Bat"?

4 What sport is played on ice and uses brooms?

5 In the game of Monopoly, from what city are the names of the properties taken?

6 In golf, what is the term for a score of one over par on a hole?

7 Who had his ear bitten by Mike Tyson in a boxing match?

8 What's the golf term for a fairway that has a sharp turn?

9 What is the lowest suit in bridge?

10 What swimmer won seven gold medals at the 1972 Summer Olympics?

Answers on page 76.

SPORTS / GAMES

MENSA SCORING

Average Mensa score:	8.475
Cumulative Mensa score in this category:	8.475

Sports and Games

11 What's the third baseman's name in the famous Abbott and Costello "Who's on First" routine?

12 What country is always first in the parade of nations at the opening ceremonies of the Summer Olympics?

13 What U.S. city has hosted the Summer Olympics twice?

14 What is the Penn State football team called?

15 What poker hand beats a straight but loses to a full house?

16 What French term is used for the person who rakes in the chips at a roulette table?

17 What Big East college do the Orangemen play for?

18 What game, whose name means "sparrow," is featured in *The Joy Luck Club*?

19 In hearts, what is it called when one player takes all the hearts and the queen of spades?

20 What sport has Marquis of Queensberry rules?

Answers on page 76.

MENSA SCORING	
Average Mensa score:	7.225
Cumulative Mensa score in this category:	15.7

Sports and Games

21 What color is the "0" pocket on a roulette wheel?

22 What is between Park Place and Boardwalk on the Monopoly board?

23 What tournament awards a green jacket to its winner?

24 What's the name of the triathlon held annually in Hawaii since 1978?

25 What is Magic Johnson's real first name?

26 What race that is over 100 years old is held annually on Patriots' Day?

27 What color is the 2 ball in pool?

28 What do the initials stand for in O. J. Simpson's name?

29 In what city is the Sugar Bowl played?

30 Who hit three home runs in a single World Series game in 1977?

Answers on page 77.

SPORTS / GAMES

MENSA SCORING

Average Mensa score:	6.025
Cumulative Mensa score in this category:	21.725

Sports and Games

31 After what tennis great is the stadium that houses the U.S. Open tennis tournament finals named?

32 Name the only team to lose four straight Super Bowls.

33 Who died in a plane crash on New Year's Eve in 1972, having collected exactly 3,000 lifetime hits?

34 For horse racing's Triple Crown, name the three races and the states in which they are run.

35 What NBA team plays its home games at the Great Western Forum?

36 What country has won the most World Cup titles?

37 What sport is divided into play periods called chukkers?

38 In the game of Yahtzee, how many points is a large straight worth?

39 Which letter in Scrabble is worth five points?

40 What color is the jersey worn by the leader of the Tour de France?

Answers on page 77.

MENSA SCORING

Average Mensa score:	4.95
Cumulative Mensa score in this category:	26.675

41 What track and field event did Dick Fosbury revolutionize?

42 What is the term for the horse-racing bet in which the first- and second-place horses are picked in the correct order?

43 In craps, what three rolls lose on the opening roll?

44 Who hit .202 with 51 RBI's and 30 stolen bases for the 1994 Class AA Birmingham Barons?

45 How many home runs did Sammy Sosa hit the year that Mark McGwire set the single-season record for home runs with 70?

46 In euchre, if spades are trump, what card is the left bower?

47 In a basketball game, what three things do you typically get 10 of in order to score a "triple-double"?

48 What is the traditional drink for the winner of the Indianapolis 500?

49 Where were the 1984 Winter Olympics held?

50 Who coached the UCLA basketball team to ten NCAA titles from 1964 to 1975?

Answers on page 77.

SPORTS/GAMES

MENSA SCORING	
Average Mensa score:	4.45
Cumulative Mensa score in this category:	31.125

51 In pinochle, what card is melded with the queen of spades to make a pinochle meld?

52 What is the name of Mario's brother in the Nintendo Super Mario Brothers games?

53 Who was the jockey that rode Whirlaway and Citation to Triple Crowns?

54 In what city is the Basketball Hall of Fame?

55 What sport has Mark Roth, Nelson Burton Jr., and Walter Ray Williams Jr. in its Hall of Fame?

56 At the 1968 Olympics, who set the long jump record that stood for over 20 years?

57 Who pitched the only perfect game in World Series history?

58 What team moved and became the Texas Rangers?

59 What team holds the record for Rose Bowl wins?

60 What's the highest number of points that can be scored with a single dart in a standard dart game?

Answers on page 77.

MENSA SCORING

Average Mensa score:	3.9
Cumulative Mensa score in this category:	35.025

Sports and Games

61 How long is the shot clock in the National Basketball Association?

62 What baseball Hall-of-Famer was nicknamed "The Splendid Splinter" and "The Kid"?

63 Who is the only three-time Super Bowl MVP?

64 Who is second to Wayne Gretzky in career goals?

65 What's the only NFL team to have an undefeated season?

66 How many points did Wilt Chamberlain score on March 2, 1962, when he set the record for most points scored in a single game?

67 What game has variations called Cricket and 501?

68 What team switched from the American League to the National League at the beginning of the 1998 season?

69 What three swords are used in fencing?

70 What's the name of the trophy awarded to the champion of the Canadian Football League?

Answers on page 78.

SPORTS/GAMES

MENSA SCORING

Average Mensa score:	3.4
Cumulative Mensa score in this category:	38.425

39

71 How many pieces are there on the board at the start of a backgammon game?

72 What position vies for the Vezina Trophy?

73 What boxer was nicknamed "The Manassa Mauler"?

74 What ballpark in baseball has the smallest seating capacity?

75 Three people have won the World Series MVP award twice. Name one.

76 In what stadium did the "Battle of the Sexes" tennis match between Bobby Riggs and Billie Jean King take place?

77 Who won the Norris Trophy every year from 1968 to 1975?

78 Who holds the record for most Gold Glove Awards for a third baseman?

79 How many yards beyond 26 miles is the length of a standard marathon race?

80 What team was home to the National League Rookie of the Year every year from 1979 to 1982 and again from 1992 to 1996?

Answers on page 78.

MENSA SCORING	
Average Mensa score:	2.825
Cumulative Mensa score in this category:	41.25

81 What is the home city of the WNBA Comets?

82 Of the hockey teams based in the U.S., which has won the most Stanley Cups?

83 What driver has won the Daytona 500 race the most times?

84 What is the name of the Montreal Expos' stadium?

85 What was the original name for the Houston Astros?

86 What two teams have faced each other three times in the Super Bowl?

87 Who was the first head coach of two different Super Bowl teams?

88 What is the name of the stadium where the French Open is played?

89 Who is the only person to win the Heisman Trophy twice?

90 What number, now retired from baseball, was worn by Jackie Robinson?

Answers on page 78.

SPORTS/GAMES

MENSA SCORING

Average Mensa score:	2.15
Cumulative Mensa score in this category:	43.4

Sports and Games

10

91 What's the highest possible score for a cribbage hand?

92 In Stratego, what are the pieces with 8's on them called?

93 What's the score given to a forfeited baseball game?

94 What pitcher holds the record for most career losses?

95 What's the name of the Major League soccer team from Chicago?

96 Who is third on the list of career home run leaders?

97 What Pittsburgh Pirates pitcher threw a perfect game for 12 innings, only to lose 1–0 in the 13th?

98 Who threw the pitch that Bobby Thomson hit for the "Shot Heard 'Round the World"?

99 Who holds the record for the most assists in the history of the NBA?

100 At casinos in Atlantic City and most other places in the U.S., how much is a green chip worth?

Answers on page 78.

MENSA SCORING

Average Mensa score:	1.525
Cumulative Mensa score in this category:	44.925

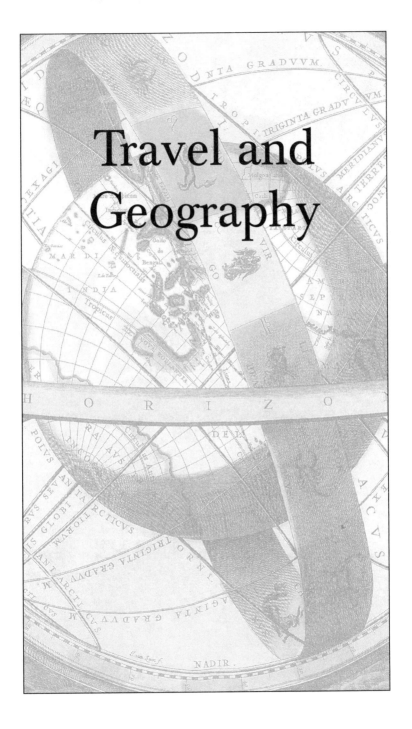

Travel and Geography

Travel and Geography

1 What city is home to the United States Naval Academy?

2 Queensland is a state in what country?

3 Halifax is the capital of what province?

4 What Pennsylvania town is famous for its Groundhog Day celebration?

5 What city was formerly called Byzantium and Constantinople?

6 What city does the "D" mint mark on pennies stand for?

7 What state elected former wrestler Jesse "The Body" Ventura as its governor?

8 What is the German name for Germany?

9 On what Hawaiian island is Honolulu located?

10 What university do Rhodes scholars attend?

Answers on page 79.

TRAVEL/GEOGRAPHY

MENSA SCORING	
Average Mensa score:	8.45
Cumulative Mensa score in this category:	8.45

Travel and Geography

11 What is the highest mountain in Africa?

12 What strait separates Spain from Morocco?

13 What 500,000-square-mile desert lies on the border of south-east Mongolia and northern China?

14 What state is home to Pikes Peak?

15 What city do people on hajjes head for?

16 What is the name of the imaginary line that runs around the Earth at 23½° south of the equator?

17 What country has "Hatikvah" as its national anthem?

18 In what state is Zion National Park?

19 Godwin Austen, the second highest mountain in the world, is also known by what letter–number combination?

20 What river does the Hoover Dam dam?

Answers on page 79.

Travel and Geography 3

21 What world capital is divided into 20 *arrondissements*?

22 What four U.S. states meet at a single point called Four Corners?

23 What is the capital of Kansas?

24 What state has "Live free or die" on its license plates?

25 What state encompasses most of Yellowstone National Park?

26 What two countries make up the island of Hispaniola?

27 What country is divided into cantons that include Uri and Zug?

28 In the 1990s, what state allowed car drivers on its interstate highways during daylight hours to go any speed that was "reasonable and prudent"?

29 What river divides Budapest into Buda and Pest?

30 What large island does the "boot" of Italy appear to be kicking?

Answers on page 80.

TRAVEL/GEOGRAPHY

Travel and Geography

31 What Canadian province is between British Columbia and Saskatchewan?

32 What mountain range is Mount Rainier a part of?

33 What is the former name of Sri Lanka?

34 What country does Greenland belong to?

35 What state is nicknamed the Pelican State?

36 What is the only three-word state capital?

37 In what city is Emory University?

38 What large island nation is north of Jamaica?

39 What is the busiest airport outside the U.S.?

40 What river runs through Rome?

Answers on page 80.

MENSA SCORING

Average Mensa score:	5.55
Cumulative Mensa score in this category:	27.4

Travel and Geography

41 What country has the zloty as its unit of currency?

42 What is the capital of Wales?

43 On what Japanese island is Tokyo located?

44 What two states are separated by the Mason-Dixon Line?

45 By what name is the country Burma now known?

46 What tiny country lies in the Pyrenees mountains between France and Spain?

47 The flag of what other country appears in the upper-left portion of the flag of Fiji?

48 What's the most populous city in Brazil?

49 What two Baltic States border Latvia?

50 Name either of the two landlocked nations found in South America.

Answers on page 80.

TRAVEL / GEOGRAPHY

MENSA SCORING	
Average Mensa score:	4.55
Cumulative Mensa score in this category:	31.95

51 What building is on the back of a $20 bill?

52 What city is the eastern terminus of the Trans-Siberian Railroad?

53 What district of Tokyo is famous for its department stores, nightclubs, and bars?

54 In what river are the Thousand Islands located?

55 What island was partially blown up in an 1883 volcanic explosion?

56 What two tiny countries are entirely surrounded by Italy?

57 What is the name of the Moorish citadel that is located in Granada, Spain?

58 What borough of New York City has the largest population?

59 What three rivers come together in Pittsburgh?

60 What three countries make up the Low Countries?

Answers on page 80.

MENSA SCORING

Average Mensa score:	4.0
Cumulative Mensa score in this category:	35.95

Travel and Geography

61 Zanzibar is a part of what country?

62 What Mexican state borders both New Mexico and Texas?

63 Which is the only U.S. state to have no highways in the Interstate Highway System?

64 What's the name of the college for the deaf located in Washington, D.C.?

65 What is the only state that has two Ivy League schools?

66 Name the capital of Romania.

67 What is the name of the only National Park in Maine?

68 What is the name of the peninsula of Denmark that connects to mainland Europe?

69 What country is called Suomi by its inhabitants?

70 What country controls the Canary Islands?

Answers on page 81.

TRAVEL/GEOGRAPHY

MENSA SCORING	
Average Mensa score:	3.575
Cumulative Mensa score in this category:	39.525

Travel and Geography

71 What country separates Honduras and Costa Rica?

72 Which of the Great Lakes has the smallest area?

73 What island in the U.S. used to be called Bedloe's Island?

74 What island forms a twin-island nation with St. Kitts?

75 What city is served by McCarran airport?

76 What is the name of the island in Paris where Notre Dame is found?

77 In what state is Skyline Drive located?

78 By what two other names was St. Petersburg formerly known?

79 What's the name of the archipelago off southern South America?

80 What tiny nation is just off the southern tip of the Malay Peninsula?

Answers on page 81.

Answers on page 81.

MENSA SCORING

Average Mensa score:	3.0
Cumulative Mensa score in this category:	42.525

81 What California island means "pelican" in Spanish?

82 What capital city is at the junction of the Blue Nile and the White Nile?

83 What's the highest mountain in the Alps?

84 What country has a flag with five sides?

85 In what country is Timbuktu located?

86 "Old Folks at Home" is the state song of what state?

87 Upper Volta is now known by what name?

88 What world capital used to be called Christiania?

89 In what state is the Grand Coulee Dam?

90 What country is entirely surrounded by South Africa?

Answers on page 81.

TRAVEL/GEOGRAPHY

MENSA SCORING

Average Mensa score:	2.25
Cumulative Mensa score in this category:	44.775

Travel and Geography

91 What country has a flag that is entirely green?

92 In what river are the Shoshone Falls?

93 What two countries are connected by the Khyber Pass?

94 What's the most populous state capital in the U.S.?

95 Rapa Nui is the lesser-known name of what island?

96 What is the least populous state in the U.S.?

97 On what island in the West Indies is the volcano Mt. Pelée located?

98 What's the longest river in Europe?

99 What is the name of the arm of the Baltic Sea that separates Sweden from Finland?

100 What country is home to the Petronas Towers (1483 feet tall)?

Answers on page 81.

MENSA SCORING

Average Mensa score:	1.5
Cumulative Mensa score in this category:	46.275

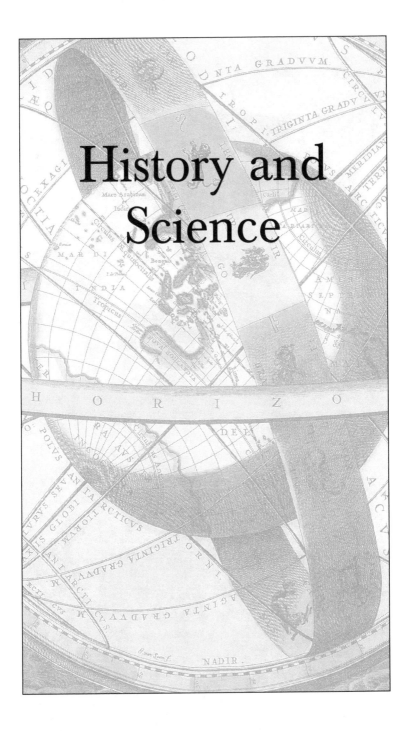

History and Science

History and Science

1 What is the familiar term for nitrous oxide?

2 What is the name of the group of megaliths on Salisbury Plain in Wiltshire, England?

3 Pure gold is how many karats?

4 What is the first day of Lent called?

5 What do the letters SCUBA stand for?

6 What constellation is known as the Winged Horse?

7 Ascorbic acid is another name for what vitamin?

8 Camp David is named after the grandson of what president?

9 What was the name of the cat in the White House during Bill Clinton's presidency?

10 Shiitake and enoki are what kind of food?

Answers on page 82.

MENSA SCORING	
Average Mensa score:	8.775
Cumulative Mensa score in this category:	8.775

History and Science

11 What element is abbreviated Pb?

12 What was the name of the B-29 bomber that dropped the atomic bomb on Hiroshima, Japan?

13 What sauce is usually used atop eggs Benedict?

14 What disease used to be called consumption?

15 What does a sphygmomanometer measure?

16 What general was known as "The Desert Fox"?

17 What language was invented by Ludwik Lejzer Zamenhof?

18 Who was the first president to be impeached?

19 What was the name of the ship on which Charles Darwin sailed in the 1860s?

20 What is the Jewish New Year called?

Answers on page 82.

MENSA SCORING

Average Mensa score:	7.725
Cumulative Mensa score in this category:	16.5

History and Science

21 Who invented dynamite?

22 What organization was George Bush the director of from 1976 to 1977?

23 Who are the four presidents depicted on Mount Rushmore?

24 What's the scientific name for the North Star?

25 What is the street address of the White House?

26 Who founded the Mormon Church?

27 What was the 48th state to enter the Union?
a) Montana b) Alaska c) Maine d) Arizona

28 What is the solid form of carbon dioxide commonly called?

29 On what date is Bastille Day celebrated in France?

30 What's the name of the political wing of the Irish Republican Army?

Answers on page 83.

MENSA SCORING	
Average Mensa score:	6.85
Cumulative Mensa score in this category:	23.35

HISTORY/SCIENCE

History and Science

31 In what year did Abraham Lincoln make his Gettysburg Address?

32 Who led an expedition on a raft called Kon-Tiki?

33 What is the familiar name of the scandal in which Albert Fall, former secretary of the interior, was convicted of accepting bribes in the leasing of the Elk Hills naval oil reserve?

34 What two presidents died on July 4, 1826?

35 Who is pictured on the $50 bill?

36 *The Watch Tower* is published by what religious group?

37 What's the technical name for the thighbone?

38 What general was nicknamed "Old Blood and Guts"?

39 The three main classes of rocks are igneous, metamorphic, and what?

40 What mineral is a 10 on the Mohs scale?

Answers on page 83.

MENSA SCORING

Average Mensa score:	6.075
Cumulative Mensa score in this category:	29.425

41 What was the name of the hill on which the Battle of Bunker Hill was fought?

42 What lowercase letter is used to represent the square root of negative one?

43 The Secret Service is part of what Cabinet department?

44 What is the Tokyo Stock Exchange index called?

45 Who was the first vice president who didn't go on to become president?
a) Alexander Hamilton b) Benjamin Franklin
c) Hannibal Hamlin d) Aaron Burr

46 What last name was shared by three vice presidents?

47 What was Millard Fillmore's political party?

48 Who fought Athens in the Peloponnesian War?

49 How old do you have to be to become a U.S. senator?

50 What's the ninth month of the Muslim calendar?

Answers on page 83.

MENSA SCORING	
Average Mensa score:	5.3
Cumulative Mensa score in this category:	34.725

HISTORY/SCIENCE

History and Science   6

51 Who was the first Secretary of State?

52 Who invented the helicopter?

53 What is the name of the person who filmed the assassination of JFK that is now a part of the National Film Registry?

54 How many pairs of chromosomes do humans have?

55 The Eightfold Path is part of what religion?

56 Who is the only person to win two elections as vice president and two as president?

57 What astrological sign follows Leo?

58 What was the name of the Siamese twin who was attached to Chang?

59 What month has amethyst as its birthstone?

60 Who was known as the Red Baron?

Answers on page 83.

Answers on page 83.

MENSA SCORING

Average Mensa score:	4.725
Cumulative Mensa score in this category:	39.45

History and Science

61 What metal coats galvanized steel?

62 Bronze is made up primarily of copper and what other metal?

63 In what country did the Battle of the Bulge take place?

64 What president was assassinated by Leon Czolgosz?

65 The disease rickets is caused by a lack of what vitamin?

66 What city has the oldest subway system in the world?

67 What president went on to serve on the Supreme Court?

68 Which president served the shortest term?

69 What was the number of the only amendment repealed from the U.S. Constitution?

70 What comes between order and genus in the taxonomic hierarchy?

Answers on page 84.

MENSA SCORING	
Average Mensa score:	3.9
Cumulative Mensa score in this category:	43.35

HISTORY/SCIENCE

History and Science

71 Who became Secretary General of the United Nations in 1997?

72 After the Vice President and Speaker of the House, who is next in line for the U.S. Presidency?

73 How many furlongs make a mile?

74 At what temperature are the Celsius and Fahrenheit temperatures the same?

75 Who was Chief Justice of the U.S. Supreme Court before William Rehnquist?

76 What is the name of the fortress city of the ancient Incans that lies about 50 miles northwest of Cuzco?

77 Who was the only president who never married?

78 Who won the 1954 Nobel Prize for chemistry as well as the 1962 Nobel Peace Prize?

79 Which planet has the most moons?

80 Who was the astronaut who accompanied Neil Armstrong and Buzz Aldrin on the first lunar mission?

Answers on page 84.

MENSA SCORING	
Average Mensa score:	3.175
Cumulative Mensa score in this category:	46.525

History and Science

81 Who wrote the three laws of planetary motion?

82 Who accompanied Edmund Hillary on his famous climb up Mount Everest?

83 What element has atomic number 3?

84 Who is known as the Mayflower Madam?

85 In what country is Alberto Fujimori the president?

86 In 1993, Eritrea declared itself independent of what nation?

87 Who beat Grover Cleveland in the 1888 election for president and then lost to him in the 1892 election?

88 What was Woodrow Wilson's real first name?

89 What was the name of the first space shuttle that flew into Earth's orbit?

90 What letter is represented by two dots in Morse code?

Answers on page 84.

Answers on page 84.

MENSA SCORING	
Average Mensa score:	2.5
Cumulative Mensa score in this category:	49.025

HISTORY/SCIENCE

91 Hibernation is the state of dormancy during the winter. What is the state of dormancy during the summer called?

92 How many electoral votes are needed to win the presidency?

93 How many stars does a major general wear?

94 As a linguistics example, who wrote "Colorless green ideas sleep furiously"?

95 Name two of the three principal Hindu deities.

96 What president was nicknamed "Old Rough and Ready"?

97 What is the lesser-known name for the more familiar brontosaurus?

98 What is the most recent year in which there wasn't a vice president for the entire calendar year?

99 The ides of a month can fall on which two dates?

100 On what date is Guy Fawkes Day celebrated?

Answers on page 84.

Brainbusters

Brainbuster 1

1 Since 1960, only five films have won for Best Picture without also capturing the Best Director award. Name two of the films.

2 What 1939 novel contains the line "Three quarks for Muster Mark!"?

3 Who declined the 1964 Nobel Prize for literature?

4 For what three teams did Nolan Ryan throw no-hitters?

5 Who is the only pitcher to throw no-hitters in back-to-back starts?

6 What country surrounds The Gambia on three sides?

7 In what state is the Buffalo National River?

8 Before George Bush, who was the most recent sitting vice president to be elected president?

9 Whom did Valerie Solanas shoot and seriously wound in 1968?

10 What city replaced Lagos as the capital of an African nation?

Answers on page 85.

MENSA SCORING	
Average Mensa score:	0.725
Cumulative Mensa score for Brainbusters:	0.725

11 John Ford holds the record for most Best Director Oscars, with four. Name two films for which he won the award.

12 What character on *The Simpsons* has three nipples?

13 What well-known composer was born on February 29, 1792?

14 What Alfred Uhry play won the 1988 Pulitzer Prize for Drama?

15 Who is the only player other than Michael Jordan to win the NBA Finals MVP two years in a row?

16 What baseball term also refers to the person who sits immediately to the right of the dealer in blackjack?

17 What was the only year in which the World Series MVP came from the losing team?

18 What state has the motto *"Oro y plata"*?

19 What game is dubbed "the classic race-ahead and bump-back game" on its box?

20 What are the three capitals of South Africa?

Answers on page 86.

MENSA SCORING	
Average Mensa score:	0.5
Cumulative Mensa score for Brainbusters:	01.225

Answers

Movies and
Television

1

1 Huey, Dewey, and Louie. [100%]
2 *The Daily Planet.* [97.5%]
3 Captain Kangaroo. [95%]
4 Green. [87.5%]
5 The Teletubbies. [85%]
6 *Home Improvement.* [80%]
7 c) Ed Bradley. [80%]
8 *Love Story.* [77.5%]
9 Jack Benny. [75%]
10 Suzanne Pleshette. [75%]

2

11 Clint Eastwood. [75%]
12 Jean-Claude Van Damme. [72.5%]
13 Cosmo. [72.5%]
14 *M*A*S*H.* [72.5%]
15 *Happy Days.* [72.5%]
16 Shirley MacLaine. [72.5%]
17 Jerry Springer. [70%]
18 Susan Sarandon. [70%]
19 Florida. [70%]
20 Richard Kimble. [67.5%]

3

21 Geraldine Jones. [67.5%]
22 Helen Hunt. [67.5%]
23 *Heidi.* [67.5%]
24 *Steamboat Willie.* [65%]
25 Grape Nehi. [65%]
26 Sean Connery. [65%]
27 Cary Grant. [65%]
28 Greg, Marcia, Peter, Jan, Bobby, Cindy. [62.5%]
29 Woody Allen. [60%]
30 Carlton. [60%]

4

31 Blythe Danner. [57.5%]
32 *The Godfather Part II.* [57.5%]
33 Vera. [55%]
34 MacGillicuddy. [55%]
35 Sensurround. [55%]
36 b) Annette Bening. [55%]
37 General Lee. [52.5%]
38 Marcel Marceau. [52.5%]
39 *Lou Grant, Phyllis,* and *Rhoda.* [52.5%]
40 Ken Burns. [52.5%]

5

41 Robert Redford. [52.5%]
42 *Bull Durham.* [52.5%]
43 Fred Grandy. [50%]
44 Jake and Elwood. [50%]
45 Garry Trudeau. [47.5%]
46 Michael Jackson. [47.5%]
47 Kim Basinger. [47.5%]
48 a) Halle Berry. [47.5%]
49 Dr. Joyce Brothers. [47.5%]
50 Gale. [45%]

6

51 *Three's Company.* [45%]
52 Kathleen Turner. [45%]
53 *The Odd Couple.* [45%]
54 *The Oprah Winfrey Show.* [45%]
55. *Heaven Can Wait.* [45%]
56 *Midnight Cowboy.* [45%]
57 Jack Russell terrier. [45%]
58 *Cosmopolitan.* [45%]
59 Kevin Costner. [45%]
60 *The Misfits.* [42.5%]

7

61 Tippi Hedren. [42.5%]
62 *Baretta.* [40%]
63 Worldwide Pants. [40%]
64 c) Alan Smithee. [40%]
65 The Munsters. [37.5%]
66 Bette Midler. [37.5%]
67 1701. [37.5%]
68 *The Six Million Dollar Man.* [35%]
69 Katharine Hepburn (*The Lion in Winter*) and Barbra Streisand (*Funny Girl*). [35%]
70 Buttermilk. [32.5%]

71 c) Little Richard. [32.5%]
72 Jennifer Aniston. [32.5%]
73 *Meet the Press.* [32.5%]
74 M (mature audience). [32.5%]
75 Tommy Lee Jones. [30%]
76 Freedonia. [30%]
77 George Clooney. [30%]
78 Melmac. [27.5%]
79 Duran Duran (now known as Duranduran). [27.5%]
80 *GoodFellas.* [27.5%]

81 Xanadu. [27.5%]
82 New York. [25%]
83 *What's Up, Tiger Lily?* [25%]
84 Paul Anka. [25%]
85 Laurence Olivier and Michael Caine. [25%]
86 Nicolas Cage. [25%]
87 *Total Recall.* [25%]
88 Uma Thurman. [22.5%]
89 "All work and no play makes Jack a dull boy." [20%]
90 Steven Spielberg, Jeffrey Katzenberg, David Geffen. [20%]

91 Chris Rock. [17.5%]
92 *Ben-Hur* and *Titanic.* [17.5%]
93 Jodie Foster. [15%]
94 *Frankie and Johnny.* [15%]
95 *It Happened One Night, One Flew Over the Cuckoo's Nest,* and *The Silence of the Lambs.* [15%]
96 *Mrs. Miniver* and *Kramer vs. Kramer.* [15%]
97 *The Godfather,* Marlon Brando (won, but refused, Best Actor Oscar), James Caan, Robert Duvall, and Al Pacino. [12.5%]
98 *Altered States.* [10%]
99 *A Room with a View.* [10%]
100 Quincy. [10%]

Music, Arts, and Letters

ANSWERS

1

1 Capulet and Montague. [92.5%]
2 Nevermore. [90%]
3 88. [90%]
4 Chattanooga Choo-Choo. [87.5%]
5 *The Merchant of Venice.* [80%]
6 Quasimodo. [75%]
7 Plié. [75%]
8 "All the News That's Fit to Print." [70%]
9 Bob Dylan. [67.5%]
10 London and Paris. [67.5%]

2

11 Michael Crichton. [67.5%]
12 Buddy Holly, Ritchie Valens, and the Big Bopper (J.P. Richardson). [65%]
13 Leviticus. [65%]
14 Baroque. [65%]
15 Maya Angelou. [62.5%]
16 Elton John. [62.5%]
17 The Spanish Civil War. [62.5%]
18 a) *The Catcher in the Rye* by J.D. Salinger. [62.5%]
19 *Uncle Tom's Cabin.* [60%]
20 Stephen King. [60%]

21 *Cabaret.* [60%]
22 *The Mousetrap* (by Agatha Christie). [57.5%]
23 *Cats.* [52.5%]
24 17. [52.5%]
25 Eagle and lion. [52.5%]
26 Frank Zappa. [52.5%]
27 Alaska, Hawaii, and Texas. [50%]
28 Claude Monet. [50%]
29 Jim Morrison. [50%]
30 Grant Wood. [50%]

31 Princess Diana. [47.5%]
32 Polly. [47.5%]
33 Milli Vanilli. [47.5%]
34 Sisyphus. [47.5%]
35 Pointillism. [47.5%]
36 Coventry, England. [42.5%]
37 *Mad.* [42.5%]
38 R.L. Stine. [42.5%]
39 *The Time Machine* (by H.G. Wells). [42.5%]
40 Dashiell Hammett. [42.5%]

41 Florence, Italy. [42.5%]
42 William Faulkner. [40%]
43 Baby, Posh, Scary, and Sporty. [40%]
44 José Carreras. [40%]
45 Cerberus. [37.5%]
46 The Hermitage. [37.5%]
47 Columbia. [37.5%]
48 Tennessee Williams. [37.5%]
49 Athena. [37.5%]
50 *La Bohème.* [37.5%]

51 Emma. [35%]
52 *The Firm* (by John Grisham). [35%]
53 Ian Fleming. [35%]
54 *The Unfinished Symphony.* [35%]
55 *Frankenstein.* [35%]
56 Napoleon. [32.5%]
57 Bob Woodward. [32.5%]
58 Leo Tolstoy. [32.5%]
59 Isadora Duncan. [32.5%]
60 Lincoln Center. [32.5%]

7

61 *La Gioconda.* [30%]
62 Grover's Corners. [30%]
63 Kurt Vonnegut Jr. [30%]
64 Modest Mussorgsky. [30%]
65 221B Baker Street. [27.5%]
66 John. [27.5%]
67 *Damn Yankees.* [27.5%]
68 Goneril, Regan, and Cordelia. [27.5%]
69 Antoine de Saint-Exupéry. [27.5%]
70 Sylvia Plath. [27.5%]

8

71 *Waiting for Godot.* [27.5%]
72 Sue Grafton. [27.5%]
73 Karen Blixen. [27.5%]
74 Gutzon Borglum. [27.5%]
75 Third. [25%]
76 Christie Brinkley. [25%]
77 I.M. Pei. [25%]
78 Agnes de Mille. [25%]
79 *The Wall Street Journal.* [22.5%]
80 Julie Andrews (in *Victor/Victoria*). [22.5%]

MUSIC/ARTS/LETTERS

9

81 Max Yasgur. [22.5%]
82 c) John Lennon. [20%]
83 "The New Colossus." [20%]
84 T.S. [20%]
85 Lucille. [17.5%]
86 West Egg. [17.5%]
87 The Red Hot Chili Peppers. [17.5%]
88 Clio. [17.5%]
89 *1984* (by George Orwell). [17.5%]
90 Salvador Dali. [15%]

10

91 *The New Yorker.* [15%]
92 Boz. [15%]
93 Antonio Gaudí. [12.5%]
94 *U.S.A.* (by John Dos Passos). [12.5%]
95 Molière. [12.5%]
96 *Anything Goes.* [12.5%]
97 *Henry IV: Part I, Henry IV: Part II,* and *The Merry Wives of Windsor.* [10%]
98 *Remembrance of Things Past* (by Marcel Proust). [10%]
99 *And to Think That I Saw It on Mulberry Street.* [10%]
100 Boopadoop. [10%]

Sports and Games

ANSWERS

1

1 Iditarod. [95%]
2 12. [90%]
3 He struck out. [90%]
4 Curling. [87.5%]
5 Atlantic City, New Jersey. [85%]
6 Bogey. [85%]
7 Evander Holyfield. [82.5%]
8 Dogleg. [77.5%]
9 Clubs. [77.5%]
10 Mark Spitz. [77.5%]

2

11 I Don't Know. [77.5%]
12 Greece. [75%]
13 Los Angeles. [75%]
14 The Nittany Lions. [72.5%]
15 Flush. [72.5%]
16 Croupier. [72.5%]
17 Syracuse University. [72.5%]
18 Mah-jongg. [70%]
19 Shooting the moon. [67.5%]
20 Boxing. [67.5%]

21 Green. [65%]
22 Luxury tax. [65%]
23 The Masters golf tournament. [65%]
24 Ironman. [62.5%]
25 Earvin. [60%]
26 The Boston Marathon. [60%]
27 Blue. [60%]
28 Orenthal James. [55%]
29 New Orleans, Louisiana. [55%]
30 Reggie Jackson. [55%]

31 Arthur Ashe. [52.5%]
32 Buffalo Bills. [50%]
33 Roberto Clemente. [50%]
34 Kentucky Derby, Kentucky; Preakness Stakes, Maryland; Belmont Stakes, New York. [50%]
35 Los Angeles Lakers. [50%]
36 Brazil (with four). [50%]
37 Polo. [50%]
38 40. [47.5%]
39 K. [47.5%]
40 Yellow. [47.5%]

41 High jump. [47.5%]
42 Exacta (or perfecta). [47.5%]
43 2, 3, and 12. [45%]
44 Michael Jordan. [45%]
45 66. [45%]
46 Jack of clubs. [45%]
47 Points, rebounds, and assists. [42.5%]
48 Milk. [42.5%]
49 Sarajevo, Yugoslavia. [42.5%]
50 John Wooden. [42.5%]

51 Jack of diamonds. [42.5%]
52 Luigi. [42.5%]
53 Eddie Arcaro. [40%]
54 Springfield, Massachusetts. [40%]
55 Bowling. [40%]
56 Bob Beamon. [37.5%]
57 Don Larsen. [37.5%]
58 Washington Senators. [37.5%]
59 University of Southern California. [37.5%]
60 60 points. [35%]

SPORTS / GAMES

61 24 seconds. [35%]
62 Ted Williams. [35%]
63 Joe Montana. [35%]
64 Gordie Howe. [35%]
65 Miami Dolphins (in 1972). [35%]
66 100 points. [35%]
67 Darts. [32.5%]
68 Milwaukee Brewers. [32.5%]
69 Saber, foil, and épée. [32.5%]
70 The Grey Cup. [32.5%]

71 30. [30%]
72 Goalie (in ice hockey). [30%]
73 Jack Dempsey. [30%]
74 Fenway Park. [30%]
75 Bob Gibson, Reggie Jackson, and Sandy Koufax. [30%]
76 The Astrodome. [27.5%]
77 Bobby Orr. [27.5%]
78 Brooks Robinson (with 16). [27.5%]
79 385. [25%]
80 Los Angeles Dodgers. [25%]

81 Houston. [25%]
82 Detroit Red Wings. [25%]
83 Richard Petty. [22.5%]
84 Olympic Stadium. [22.5%]
85 Houston Colt .45's. [22.5%]
86 Pittsburgh Steelers and Dallas Cowboys. [20%]
87 Don Shula (Baltimore Colts and Miami Dolphins). [20%]
88 Roland Garros. [20%]
89 Archie Griffin. [20%]
90 42. [17.5%]

91 29. [17.5%]
92 Miners. [17.5%]
93 9–0. [17.5%]
94 Cy Young. [17.5%]
95 Fire. [17.5%]
96 Willie Mays. [15%]
97 Harvey Haddix. [12.5%]
98 Ralph Branca. [12.5%]
99 John Stockton. [12.5%]
100 $25. [12.5%]

Travel and Geography

ANSWERS

1

1 Annapolis, Maryland. [90%]
2 Australia. [90%]
3 Nova Scotia. [90%]
4 Punxsutawney. [85%]
5 Instanbul, Turkey. [85%]
6 Denver. [85%]
7 Minnesota. [82.5%]
8 Deutschland. [82.5%]
9 Oahu. [77.5%]
10 Oxford. [77.5%]

2

11 Mount Kilimanjaro. [75%]
12 Gibraltar. [75%]
13 Gobi. [72.5%]
14 Colorado. [72.5%]
15 Mecca, Saudi Arabia. [72.5%]
16 Tropic of Capricorn. [72.5%]
17 Israel. [70%]
18 Utah. [67.5%]
19 K2. [67.5%]
20 Colorado. [67.5%]

21 Paris. [67.5%]

22 Arizona, Colorado, New Mexico, and Utah. [65%]

23 Topeka. [65%]

24 New Hampshire. [62.5%]

25 Wyoming. [62.5%]

26 Dominican Republic and Haiti. [62.5%]

27 Switzerland. [62.5%]

28 Montana. [60%]

29 Danube. [60%]

30 Sicily. [60%]

31 Alberta. [57.5%]

32 The Cascades. [57.5%]

33 Ceylon. [57.5%]

34 Denmark. [55%]

35 Louisiana. [55%]

36 Salt Lake City. [55%]

37 Atlanta, Georgia. [55%]

38 Cuba. [55%]

39 Heathrow (in London). [55%]

40 Tiber. [52.5%]

41 Poland. [50%]

42 Cardiff. [50%]

43 Honshu. [50%]

44 Pennsylvania and Maryland. [45%]

45 Myanmar. [45%]

46 Andorra. [45%]

47 United Kingdom. [42.5%]

48 São Paulo. [42.5%]

49 Estonia and Lithuania. [42.5%]

50 Bolivia and Paraguay. [42.5%]

51 The White House. [40%]

52 Vladivostok. [40%]

53 The Ginza. [40%]

54 St. Lawrence. [40%]

55 Krakatoa. [40%]

56 San Marino and Vatican City. [40%]

57 Alhambra. [40%]

58 Brooklyn. [40%]

59 Ohio, Allegheny, and Monongahela. [40%]

60 Belgium, the Netherlands, and Luxembourg. [40%]

61 Tanzania. [37.5%]

62 Chihuahua. [37.5%]

63 Alaska. [37.5%]

64 Gallaudet College. [35%]

65 New York (Columbia and Cornell). [35%]

66 Bucharest. [35%]

67 Acadia. [35%]

68 Jutland. [35%]

69 Finland. [35%]

70 Spain. [35%]

71 Nicaragua. [32.5%]

72 Ontario. [32.5%]

73 Liberty Island. [30%]

74 Nevis. [30%]

75 Las Vegas. [30%]

76 Île de la Cité. [30%]

77 Virginia. [30%]

78 Petrograd and Leningrad. [30%]

79 Tierra del Fuego. [27.5%]

80 Singapore. [27.5%]

81 Alcatraz. [27.5%]

82 Khartoum, Sudan. [25%]

83 Mont Blanc. [25%]

84 Nepal. [22.5%]

85 Mali. [22.5%]

86 Florida. [22.5%]

87 Burkina Faso. [20%]

88 Oslo. [20%]

89 Washington. [20%]

90 Lesotho. [20%]

91 Libya. [17.5%]

92 Snake River. [17.5%]

93 Pakistan and Afghanistan. [17.5%]

94 Phoenix, Arizona. [15%]

95 Easter Island. [15%]

96 Wyoming. [15%]

97 Martinique. [15%]

98 Volga. [15%]

99 Gulf of Bothnia. [12.5%]

100 Malaysia. [10%]

TRAVEL/GEOGRAPHY

History and Science

1

1 Laughing gas. [100%]
2 Stonehenge. [92.5%]
3 24. [87.5%]
4 Ash Wednesday. [87.5%]
5 Self-contained underwater breathing apparatus. [85%]
6 Pegasus. [85%]
7 Vitamin C. [85%]
8 Dwight D. Eisenhower. [85%]
9 Socks. [85%]
10 Mushrooms. [85%]

2

11 Lead. [82.5%]
12 *Enola Gay.* [82.5%]
13 Hollandaise sauce. [80%]
14 Tuberculosis. [80%]
15 Blood pressure. [75%]
16 Erwin Rommel. [75%]
17 Esperanto. [75%]
18 Andrew Johnson. [75%]
19 *Beagle.* [75%]
20 Rosh Hashanah. [72.5%]

3

21 Alfred Nobel. [72.5%]
22 The CIA. [72.5%]
23 George Washington,
   Thomas Jefferson,
   Abraham Lincoln, and
   Theodore Roosevelt. [70%]
24 Polaris. [70%]
25 1600 Pennsylvania
   Avenue. [67.5%]
26 Joseph Smith. [67.5%]
27 d) Arizona. [67.5%]
28 Dry ice. [67.5%]
29 July 14. [65%]
30 Sinn Fein. [65%]

31 1863. [62.5%]
32 Thor Heyerdahl. [62.5%]
33 Teapot Dome. [62.5%]
34 John Adams and Thomas
   Jefferson. [62.5%]
35 Ulysses S. Grant. [60%]
36 Jehovah's Witnesses. [60%]
37 Femur. [60%]
38 George S. Patton. [60%]
39 Sedimentary. [60%]
40 Diamond. [57.5%]

41 Breed's Hill. [57.5%]
42 i. [55%]
43 Treasury Department.
   [55%]
44 Nikkei. [55%]
45 d) Aaron Burr. [55%]
46 Johnson (Richard, Andrew,
   and Lyndon). [52.5%]
47 Whig. [52.5%]
48 Sparta. [50%]
49 30. [50%]
50 Ramadan. [47.5%]

51 Thomas Jefferson. [47.5%]
52 Igor Sikorsky. [47.5%]
53 Abraham Zapruder.
   [47.5%]
54 23. [47.5%]
55 Buddhism. [47.5%]
56 Richard Nixon. [47.5%]
57 Virgo. [47.5%]
58 Eng. [47.5%]
59 February. [47.5%]
60 Manfred von Richthofen.
   [45%]

61 Zinc. [42.5%]

62 Tin. [42.5%]

63 Belgium. [42.5%]

64 William McKinley. [42.5%]

65 Vitamin D. [40%]

66 London. [37.5%]

67 William Howard Taft. [37.5%]

68 William Henry Harrison (31 days). [35%]

69 18th (Prohibition). [35%]

70 Family. [35%]

71 Kofi Annan. [32.5%]

72 President pro tempore of the Senate. [32.5%]

73 Eight. [32.5%]

74 –40. [32.5%]

75 Warren Burger. [32.5%]

76 Machu Picchu. [32.5%]

77 James Buchanan. [32.5%]

78 Linus Pauling. [30%]

79 Saturn. [30%]

80 Michael Collins. [30%]

81 Johannes Kepler. [30%]

82 Tenzing Norgay. [27.5%]

83 Lithium. [27.5%]

84 Sidney Biddle Barrows. [27.5%]

85 Peru. [25%]

86 Ethiopia. [25%]

87 Benjamin Harrison. [22.5%]

88 Thomas. [22.5%]

89 *Columbia.* [22.5%]

90 I. [20%]

91 Estivation. [20%]

92 270. [20%]

93 Two. [17.5%]

94 Noam Chomsky. [17.5%]

95 Brahma, Shiva (or Siva), and Vishnu. [17.5%]

96 Zachary Taylor. [17.5%]

97 Apatosaurus. [15%]

98 1964. [12.5%]

99 13th or 15th. [12.5%]

100 November 5. [10%]

Brainbusters

ANSWERS

1 *In the Heat of the Night* (Mike Nichols won for *The Graduate*), *The Godfather* (Bob Fosse won for *Cabaret*), *Chariots of Fire* (Warren Beatty won for *Reds*), *Driving Miss Daisy* (Oliver Stone won for *Born on the Fourth of July*), and *Shakespeare in Love* (Steven Spielberg won for *Saving Private Ryan*). [7.5%]

2 *Finnegans Wake.* [7.5%]

3 Jean-Paul Sartre. [7.5%]

4 Houston Astros, California Angels, and Texas Rangers. [7.5%]

5 Johnny Vander Meer. [7.5%]

6 Senegal. [7.5%]

7 Arkansas. [7.5%]

8 Martin Van Buren. [7.5%]

9 Andy Warhol. [7.5%]

10 Abuja, Nigeria. [5%]

11 *The Informer, The Grapes of Wrath, How Green Was My Valley,* and *The Quiet Man.* [5%]

12 Krusty the Clown. [5%]

13 Gioacchino Rossini. [5%]

14 *Driving Miss Daisy.* [5%]

15 Hakeem Olajuwon. [5%]

16 Third base. [5%]

17 1960 (Bobby Richardson of the Yankees won the award, but the Pirates won the Series). [5%]

18 Montana. [5%]

19 Trouble. [5%]

20 Cape Town, Pretoria, and Bloemfontein. [5%]

Index

To look up again your favorite questions
...and to test friends.

Abbott and Costello routine, 34 (11)
Africa, 46 (11)
Airport, busiest, 48 (39)
A.L. to N.L. team, 39 (68)
Alaskan sled dog race, 33 (1)
ALF, 16 (78)
Alps, 53 (83)
A.M. Chicago, 14 (54)
American Gothic painter, 23 (30)
Amethyst, 62 (59)
Andromeda Strain, 22 (11)
Animal Farm, 26 (56)
Annie Savoy movie line, 13 (42)
Arrondissements, 47 (21)
Ascorbic acid, 57 (7)
Assassin Leon Czolgosz, 63 (64)
Astrological sign, 62 (57)
Astronaut, one of three, 64 (80)
Athens's Peloponnesian foe, 61 (48)
Atomic number 3, 65 (83)
Awards
  Emmy, Best Actress
    Comedy 1996–97, 11 (22)
  Oscar actor nominations
    (four), 18 (97)

Oscar, Best Actress 1997, 11 (22)
Oscar, Best Actress tie 1968, 15 (69)
Oscar, Best Director, earlier "corpse," 14 (59)
Oscar, Best Director, in debut, 13 (41)
Oscar, Best Picture, but..., 67 (1)
Oscar, Best Picture (movie sequel), 12 (32)
Oscar, Best Picture title abbr., 18 (96)
Oscar, Best Picture, X-rated, 14 (56)
Oscar-winning Gore "roomie," 16 (75)
Oscar wins (eleven), 18 (92)
Oscar wins, five top, 18 (95)

B.B. King, 29 (85)
Backgammon, 40 (71)
Ballet move, 21 (7)
Baltic Sea arm, 54 (99)
Baltic States, 49 (49)
Barbarella, 16 (79)
Baseball, 37 (45), 39 (62), 39 (68), 40 (74), 42 (93), 42 (94), 42 (96)
Baseball/blackjack term, 68 (16)

Index key: page (question number)

87

Basketball, 37 (47), 37 (50), 38 (54), 39 (61)
Bastille "day," 59 (29)
Batman Returns, 12 (36)
Battle of Bunker Hill, 61 (41)
Battle of the Bulge, 63 (63)
"Battle of the Sexes" match, 40 (76)
Bedloe's Island, 52 (73)
Beethoven Eroica aka, 28 (75)
Bible book, 22 (13)
Big Chill, 14 (59)
Bill Clinton
  inauguration poem, 22 (15)
  White House cat, 57 (9)
Billie Jean King and Bobby Riggs, 40 (76)
Birmingham Barons, 37 (44)
Blackjack, 68 (16)
Blondie Bumstead, 30 (100)
Blue and White Nile junction, 53 (82)
Blues Brothers, 13 (44)
Bob Keeshan, 9 (3)
Bob Newhart Show, 9 (10)
Bowling perfect game, 33 (2)
Brady Bunch, 11 (28)
Braselton, Georgia, purchase of, 13 (47)
Brazil, 49 (48)
Bribe scandal of Elk Hills, 60 (33)
Bridge low suit, 33 (9)
Brontosaurus aka, 66 (97)
Bronze, 63 (62)
Bruce Willis/Demi Moore marriage, 16 (71)
"Brussels, Muscles from," 10 (12)
Budapest, 47 (29)
Buffalo National River, 67 (7)

Burma, 49 (45)
Burt Reynolds, 14 (58)
Byzantium, 45 (5)

Camp David, 57 (8)
Canada province, 48 (31)
Canadian Football League, 39 (70)
Canary Islands, 51 (70)
Carbon dioxide as solid, 59 (28)
"Casey at the Bat," 33 (3)
Casino "green," 42 (100)
Catwoman, *not!*, 12 (36)
Charles Darwin, 58 (19)
Charles Dickens aka, 30 (92)
Cheers, 12 (33)
Chitty Chitty Bang Bang, 26 (53)
Christiania, 53 (88)
Chromosomes, 62 (54)
Chukkers, 36 (37)
"Church of Baseball," 13 (42)
Citation jockey, 38 (53)
Citizen Kane, 17 (81)
Civil War, 12 (40)
"Clair de Lune," 18 (94)
Clarinet-playing director, 11 (29)
Clark Gable final film, 14 (60)
Clark Kent, 9 (2)
Composer's birth, 68 (13)
Constantinople, 45 (5)
Constitution repeal, 63 (69)
Consumption, 58 (14)
Costa Rica and Honduras, 52 (71)
Craps, 37 (43)
Cribbage, 42 (91)
Cricket and 501, 39 (67)
Cyborg, 15 (68)

"D" mint mark, 45 (6)

Daily paper record holder, 28 (79)

Dale Evans's horse, 15 (70)

Dart score, 38 (60)

Daytona 500, 41 (83)

Death
air crash New Year's Eve, 36 (33)
Astapovo railway junction, 26 (58)
by scarf, 26 (59)
in Paris bathtub, 23 (29)
three in air crash, 22 (12)
two presidents, 60 (34)

Demi Moore, 16 (71)

Denmark peninsula, 51 (68)

Desert, 46 (13)

"Desert Fox," 58 (16)

Dick Fosbury, 37 (41)

Dodge Charger name, 12 (37)

Donald Duck, 9 (1)

Dr. Seuss, 30 (99)

Dreamworks SKG, 17 (90)

Drew Barrymore debut, 18 (98)

Driving speed "laissez faire," 47 (28)

Duck Soup, 16 (76)

Dukes of Hazzard, 12 (37)

Dynamite, 59 (21)

E/R and *ER* doctor, 16 (77)

Earthquake effect feature, 12 (35)

Egg Pictures, 18 (93)

Eggs Benedict, 58 (13)

Eightfold Path, 62 (55)

Electoral votes, 66 (92)

Elizabeth Taylor, 13 (46)

Eloi and Morlocks, 24 (39)

Emory University, 48 (37)

Enoki and Shiitake, 57 (10)

Enterprise (original), NCC number, 15 (67)

Eritrea, 65 (86)

Estragon and Vladimir, 28 (71)

Ethan Hawke, 17 (88)

Euchre, 37 (46)

Europe river, 54 (98)

Eustace Tilly annual event, 30 (91)

"Eye on the Sparrow" theme, 15 (62)

Fabrice Morvan, 24 (33)

Falstaff, 30 (97)

Fencing, 39 (69)

$50-bill personage, 60 (35)

Fiji flag, 49 (47)

Film "fake name," 15 (64)

Flag
five-sided, 53 (84)
green, 54 (91)

Flea, 29 (87)

Flip Wilson, 11 (21)

Football Oakland/Jets cutaway, 11 (23)

Forfeit, 42 (93)

42nd Parallel, 1919, and *Big Money* trilogy, 30 (94)

48th state, 59 (27)

Four Corners, 47 (22)

Frasier's Eddie, 14 (57)

French Open, 41 (88)

Fugitive, 10 (20)

Furlong, 64 (73)

Gala artist, 29 (90)

Galvanized steel coating, 63 (61)

Gambia, 67 (6)
George Bush, 59 (22), 67 (8)
Germany, 45 (8)
Gettysburg Address, 60 (31)
Godwin Austen, 46 (19)
Gold Glove Award, 40 (78)
Gold rating, 57 (3)
Golf
  score, 33 (6)
  "sharp turn" term, 33 (8)
"Goodbye, Farewell, Amen,"
  10 (14)
Goodbye to Berlin, 23 (21)
Goosebumps, 24 (38)
Granada citadel, 50 (57)
Grand Coulee Dam, 53 (89)
Great Gatsby, 29 (86)
Great Lakes, 52 (72)
Green jacket, 35 (23)
Greenland, 48 (34)
Griffin mix, 23 (25)
Groundhog Day, 45 (4)
Guy Fawkes Day, 66 (100)
Gwyneth Paltrow relative 12
  (31)

Hades's three-headed guard
  dog, 25 (45)
Haiku syllables, 23 (24)
Hajjes, 46 (15)
Halifax, 45 (3)
Hall of Fame, 38 (55)
  Basketball, 38 (54)
"Hatikvah," 46 (17)
Hearts play, 34 (19)
Heisman Trophy, 41 (89)
Helicopter, 62 (52)
Here Comes Mr. Jordan, 14 (55)
Hindu deities, 66 (95)
Hiroshima bomber, 58 (12)
Hispaniola, 47 (26)

History muse, 29 (88)
Honduras and Costa Rica, 52
  (71)
Honolulu, 45 (9)
Hoover Dam, 46 (20)
Horse-racing bet, 37 (42)
Houston Astros, 41 (85)
Hunchback of Notre Dame, 21 (6)

I Dream of Jeannie, 10 (19)
I Love Lucy, 12 (34)
"Ice and brooms" game, 33 (4)
Ides dates, 66 (99)
Impression: Sunrise painter, 23
  (28)
Incans' fortress city, 64 (76)
Indianapolis 500, 37 (48)
Irish Republic Army wing, 59
  (30)
Isak Dinesen aka, 28 (73)
Island explosion, 50 (55)
Italy, 50 (56)
  "bootee," 47 (30)
Ivy League, 51 (65)

Jackie Robinson, 41 (90)
Jamaica neighbor, 48 (38)
James A. Michener "state"
  tomes, 23 (27)
Jane Pauley relative, 13 (45)
Jean Baptiste Poquelin aka, 30
  (95)
Jesse Ventura, 45 (7)
Jewish New Year, 58 (20)
JFK assassination filmer, 62
  (53)
John Belushi bio *Wired*, 26 (57)
John Ford Best Director Oscar
  wins, 68 (11)
Johnny Carson, love song to,
  15 (66)

"Johnny's Theme," 17 (84)
"Joke and Dagger," 24 (37)
Joy Luck Club game, 34 (18)

Kansas, 47 (23)
Khyber Pass, 54 (93)
Kilgore Trout writer, 27 (63)
"Killer" drag character, 11 (21)
King Lear's daughters, 27 (68)
Kinsey Millhone, 28 (72)
Kon-Tiki, 60 (32)
Kramer on *Seinfeld*, 10 (13)

Lady Godiva, 24 (36)
Lagos replacement, 67 (10)
Language by Zamenhof, 58 (17)
Larry Fortensky, 13 (46)
Late Show with David Letterman, 15 (63)
Lazarus's "Statue of Liberty" poem, 29 (83)
Lent begins, 57 (4)
Line at South 23½°, 46 (16)
Linguistics "sentence," 66 (94)
Little Prince, 27 (69)
"Live free or die," 47 (24)
Long jump, 38 (56)
Love Boat, 13 (43)
Low Countries, 50 (60)

*M*A*S*H*, 11 (25)
Madame Bovary, 26 (51)
Made Men, 16 (80)
Madeleine, a novel treat, 30 (98)
"Magic" Johnson, né, 35 (25)
Maine National Park, 51 (67)
Major general's stars, 66 (93)
Malay Peninsula, 52 (80)
"Manassa Mauler," 40 (73)

Marathon, 40 (79)
Marilyn Monroe final film, 14 (60)
Marquis of Queensberry rules, 34 (20)
Mary Tyler Moore Show spinoffs, 12 (39)
Mason-Dixon Line, 49 (44)
Mayflower Madam, 65 (84)
Mayor
  of Carmel, 10 (11)
  of Cincinnati, 10 (17)
McCarran airport, 52 (75)
Mel Brooks, 12 (38)
Melanie Griffith's relative, 15 (61)
Metropolitan Opera complex, 26 (60)
Mexico, 51 (62)
Mickey Mouse, 11 (24)
Millard Fillmore party, 61 (47)
Minerva, Greek version, 25 (49)
Miss USA first runner-up 1986, 13 (48)
Mitch McDeere, 26 (52)
"Modern Prometheus" novel, 26 (55)
Mohs 10, 60 (40)
Mona Lisa aka, 27 (61)
Monopoly
  "names," 33 (5)
  site, 35 (22)
Montreal Expos stadium, 41 (84)
Mork, appearance of, 10 (15)
Morlocks and Eloi, 24 (39)
Mormon Church, 59 (26)
Morse code letter, 65 (90)
Mothers of Invention, 23 (26)

Mount
  Everest climber, 65 (82)
  Rainier, 48 (32)
  Rushmore creator, 28 (74)
  Rushmore presidents, 59
    (23)
Movie ratings, 16 (74)
Mr. Magoo, 18 (100)
Mr. Universe, Scottish
  competitor, 11 (26)
Mt. Pelée, 54 (97)
Musical period, 22 (14)
Muslim month, 61 (50)
"Muster Mark" novel, 67 (2)
Mythic stone roller, 24 (34)

Name change
  Archibald Leach, 11 (27)
  Reginald Dwight, 22 (16)
  Robert Zimmerman, 21 (9)
NBA, 36 (35), 42 (99)
  Finals MVP, 68 (15)
New York City, 50 (58)
New York Times slogan, 21 (8)
Newhart, 9 (10)
NFL record, 39 (65)
Night of the Iguana, 25 (48)
Nike's "Li'l Penny," 18 (91)
Nile, 53 (82)
Nitrous oxide, 57 (1)
N.L. Rookie of the Year, 40
  (80)
Nobel Prize
  decliner, 67 (3)
  winner, 64 (78)
Nolan Ryan no-hitters, 67 (4)
Norris Trophy, 40 (77)
North Star, 59 (24)
Notre Dame cathedral, 52
  (76)
Nude centerfold, 14 (58)

O.J. Simpson, 35 (28)
Oklahoma choreographer, 28
  (78)
"Old Blood and Guts," 60 (38)
"Old Folks at Home," 53 (86)
Oliver's Story, 9 (8)
Olympics, Summer
  first nation in parade, 34 (12)
  gold-medal swimmer, 33 (10)
  long jump, 38 (56)
  twice U.S. host city, 34 (13)
Orangemen, 34 (17)
Ordinary People, 13 (41)
Our Town's town, 27 (62)

Patriots' Day race, 35 (26)
Pb, 58 (11)
"Pelican" island, 53 (81)
Pelican State, 48 (35)
Penn State team, 34 (14)
Penn Station train, 21 (4)
People "coverage," 24 (31)
Petronas Towers, 54 (100)
Phillip K. Dick, 17 (87)
Piano keys, 21 (3)
Picasso's *Guernica* war, 22 (17)
Pictures at an Exhibition, 27 (64)
Pigeon, Cecily and
  Gwendolyn, 14 (53)
Pikes Peak, 46 (14)
Pinochle, 38 (51)
Pitcher, no-hitters back to
  back, 67 (5)
Pittsburgh Pirates, 42 (97)
Pittsburgh rivers, 50 (59)
Planet with most moons, 64
  (79)
Planetary motion laws, 65 (81)
Play
  record in London, 23 (22)
  record on Broadway, 23 (23)

Poker hand, 34 (15)
Pool 2 ball, 35 (27)
Presidency, won over/lost to
    Cleveland, 65 (87)
President Fujimori, 65 (85)
President, U.S.
  impeached, 58 (18)
  never married, 64 (77)
  next in line for, 64 (72)
  "Old Rough and Ready," 66
    (96)
  shortest term, 63 (68)
  then Supreme Court, 63 (67)
  two same-day deaths, 60 (34)
Pulitzer Prize administrator,
    25 (47)
Pyrenees nation, 49 (46)

Queensland, 45 (2)

"Race ahead/bump back"
    game, 68 (19)
Rapa Nui, 54 (95)
"Raven," 21 (2)
Red Baron, 62 (60)
Regal Beagle, 14 (51)
Rent base, 25 (50)
Rhoda, 11 (30)
Rhodes scholar, 45 (10)
Richard Bachman aka, 22 (20)
Rickets, 63 (65)
River of Dreams album designer,
    28 (76)
Rob Pilatus, 24 (33)
Rochester, 9 (9)
Rock and Roll Hall of Fame
    and Museum, 28 (77)
Rock classes, 60 (39)
Rocky Horror Picture Show, 10
    (18)
Rolling Stone cover, 29 (82)

Romania, 51 (66)
Rome river, 48 (40)
Romeo and Juliet families, 21 (1)
Rose Bowl, 38 (59)
Roulette
  "chipster," 34 (16)
  "0" pocket, 35 (21)

Sagrada Familia church, 30 (93)
Salisbury Plain megaliths, 57
    (2)
Sam Spade, 24 (40)
Sammy Sosa, 37 (45)
Schubert's *Symphony No. 8 in B
    minor*, 26 (54)
Scrabble, 36 (39)
SCUBA, 57 (5)
Secret Service, 61 (43)
Secretary of State, 62 (51)
Senator, age requirement, 61
    (49)
Seurat's *Sunday Afternoon…*, 24
    (35)
Shakespeare line titles, 22 (18)
Sherlock Holmes
  address, 27 (65)
  Watson's first name, 27 (66)
Shiitake and enoki, 57 (10)
Shining, 17 (89)
Shoshone Falls, 54 (92)
"Shot Heard" pitcher, 42 (98)
Shylock, 21 (5)
Siamese twin of Chang, 62 (58)
Silent Movie speaking part, 12
    (38)
Simon Legree, 22 (19)
Simpsons, 68 (12)
"Six months…" opener, 27 (66)
60 Minutes, 9 (7)
$64,000 Question and *Challenge*,
    13 (49)

Skyline Drive, 52 (77)
Sleuth, 17 (85)
Soccer team (Chicago), 42 (95)
South Africa, 53 (90), 68 (20)
South America, 49 (50), 52 (79)
Space shuttle, 65 (89)
Spain/Morocco, 46 (12)
Sphygmomanometer, 58 (15)
Spice Girls, 25 (43)
Square root of negative one,
    61 (42)
Sri Lanka, 48 (33)
St. Kitts, 52 (74)
St. Petersburg, 25 (46), 52 (78)
Stanley Cup, 41 (82)
Star Trek, 9 (4), 15 (67)
State motto, 68 (18)
Stratego, 42 (92)
"Striking thirteen" novel, 29
    (89)
Subway, oldest, 63 (66)
Sugar Bowl city, 35 (29)
Summer dormancy, 66 (91)
Suomi, 51 (69)
Super Bowl, 36 (32), 39 (63),
    41 (86), 41 (87)
Super Mario's bro, 38 (52)
Supreme Court Chief Justice,
    64 (75)

Tale of Two Cities, 21 (10)
Talia Shire relative, 17 (86)
Taxonomic hierarchy, 63 (70)
Ted Hughes's poet wife, 27 (70)
Telly Savalas and Friend, 16
    (72)
Television show, longest-
    running, 16 (73)
Temperature same, 64 (74)
Terrence McNally, 18 (94)
Texas Rangers, 38 (58)

Thighbone, 60 (37)
1313 Mockingbird Lane, 15 (65)
Thousand Islands, 50 (54)
Three Tenors, 25 (44)
Timbuktu, 53 (85)
Tinky Winky, 9 (5)
Tokyo, 49 (43), 50 (53)
    Stock Exchange, 61 (44)
Tom Sawyer's relative, 24 (32)
Tony *no*-minee, 28 (80)
Tool Time, 9 (6)
Tour de France, 36 (40)
Track and field, 37 (41)
Trans-Siberian Railroad, 50
    (52)
Triathlon, 35 (24)
Triple Crown, 36 (34), 38 (53)
$20-bill building, 50 (51)
Tyson attack, 33 (7)

UCLA coach, 37 (50)
Uffizi Gallery, 25 (41)
Uhry Pulitzer Prize winner, 68
    (14)
U.N. Secretary General, 64 (71)
United States Naval Academy,
    45 (1)
Upper Volta, 53 (87)
Uri and Zug, 47 (27)
U.S. Interstate Highway
    System, 51 (63)
U.S. Open stadium, 36 (31)
U.S. state, 54 (96)
    capital, 48 (36), 54 (94)

Valerie Solanas, 67 (9)
Vanessa Williams, 17 (82)
Vezina Trophy, 40 (72)
Vice President
    absent for year, 66 (98)
    and President twice, 62 (56)

94

dead-end job, 61 (45)

last names, 61 (46)

"Visit to Florence" title, 18 (99)

Vladimir and Estragon, 28 (71)

Wales, 49 (42)

Warren Beatty relative, 10 (16)

Washington D.C. college for deaf, 51 (64)

Watch Tower, 60 (36)

Wayne Gretzky runner-up, 39 (64)

Whirlaway jockey, 38 (53)

White House address, 59 (25)

Who Framed Roger Rabbit, 14 (52)

"Who's on First," 34 (11)

William Hurt debut, 18 (98)

Wilt Chamberlain, 39 (66)

Winged Horse, 57 (6)

Winter Olympics, 37 (49)

Wizard of Oz, 13 (50)

WNBA Comets, 41 (81)

Woodrow Wilson's name, 65 (88)

Woodstock landowner, 29 (81)

Woody Allen "recipe" movie, 17 (83)

World According to Garp, 29 (84)

World Cup, 36 (36)

World Series

home runs, 35 (30)

MVP, 40 (75), 68 (17)

perfect game, 38 (57)

Yahtzee, 36 (38)

Yellowstone National Park, 47 (25)

Yoknapatawpha County, 25 (42)

"You're the Top," 30 (96)

Zanzibar, 51 (61)

Zion National Park, 46 (18)

Zloty, 49 (41)

Zug and Uri, 47 (27)

What Is American Mensa?

American Mensa ● The High IQ Society

One out of 50 people qualifies for American Mensa...
Are *you* the One?

American Mensa, Ltd., is an organization for individuals who have one common trait: a score in the top two percent of the population on a standardized intelligence test. Over five million Americans are eligible for membership...you may be one of them.

Looking for intellectual stimulation? You'll find a good "mental workout" in the *Mensa Bulletin*, our national magazine. Voice your opinion in the newsletter published by your local group, and attend activities and gatherings with fascinating programs and engaging conversation.

Looking for social interaction? There's something happening on the Mensa calendar almost daily. Events range from lectures to game nights to parties. Each year, there are over 40 regional gatherings and an Annual Gathering, where you can meet people, exchange ideas, and make interesting new friends.

Looking for others who share your special interest? Whatever your interest may be—computer gaming, Monty Python, or scuba—there's probably a Mensa Special Interest Group (SIG) for you. There are over 150 SIGs, which are started and maintained by members.

So contact us today for a free brochure and application:

American Mensa, Ltd., 1229 Corporate Drive West, Arlington, TX 76006 (800) 66-MENSA AmericanMensa@compuserve.com http://www.us.mensa.org (If you do not live in the U.S., you can contact your national Mensa society via: Mensa International, 15 The Ivories, 6–8 Northampton St., Islington, London N1 2HY England.)